Published by arrangement with Loewe Verlag GmbH.

Title of the original German edition: *Was mach ich nur mit meiner Trauer?*
© 2018 Loewe Verlag GmhH, Bindlach

Sky Pony Press books may be purchased in bulk at special discounts for sales promotion, corporate gifts, fund-raising, or educational purposes. Special editions can also be created to specifications. For details, contact the Special Sales Department, Sky Pony Press, 307 West 36th Street, 11th Floor, New York, NY 10018 or info@skyhorsepublishing.com.

Sky Pony® is a registered trademark of Skyhorse Publishing, Inc.®, a Delaware corporation.

Visit our website at www.skyponypress.com.

10 9 8 7 6 5 4 3 2 1

Manufactured in China, November 2019
This product conforms to CPSIA 2008

Library of Congress Cataloging-in-Publication Data is available on file.

Cover provided by Loewe Verlag GmbH
Cover illustration by Dagmar Geisler

Print ISBN: 978-1-5107-4658-9
Ebook ISBN: 978-1-5107-4669-5

# What to Do When I Am Sad

Written and Illustrated by
**Dagmar Geisler**

Translated by
**Andrea Jones Berasaluce**

Sky Pony Press
New York

Have you ever been sad?

There are many reasons
why someone can be sad.

What does it feel like to be sad?

And I would love to scream very loudly.

It feels like I have a stomachache.

And then I have no desire to do anything.

Every person is sad in their own way.
Everyone can experience it differently.
And it doesn't always feel the same
every time you're sad, either.

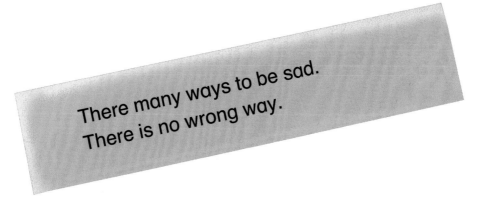

There many ways to be sad.
There is no wrong way.

A couple of questions that can help you:

What is the reason for my grief?

Is my sadness big or small?

Is there only one reason for it or are there maybe more?

Do I need someone to comfort me?

Or would I rather be alone?

Would it be easier if I tell someone what's making me sad?

Whom should I tell? Mom or Dad? Or maybe just my stuffed animal?

Is there anything that would help me feel better now? Maybe a hot chocolate or a nice story? Or an afternoon snuggled on the couch or playing a game outdoors, in the fresh air. . . ?

Can you think of any other questions you can ask yourself?

One event that makes
people sad is losing a loved one.

Everything that lives must at some point
die; this is our life cycle, and it's per-
fectly normal. That's what happens
with flowers that bloom in summer.
In autumn, they hang their heads.
At this time, leaves on the trees
sail to the ground and then
winter comes.

SPRING

WINTER

Water

The wind carries away the seeds

A seed grows in the earth

We know that in spring, new flowers grow and that trees become green again. But if we loved this particular flower so, it makes us sad nevertheless.

We human beings, of course, live much longer than flowers. And we make memories throughout the years.

SUMMER

A bud

Sun

New seeds

The dead leaves return to the earth

AUTUMN

This is a long
time ago:

Great-grandma
as a kid
←

Great-grandma
during the harvest

But at some point, every person must go.

Like, for example, Marie's great-grandmother. She had almost turned one hundred years old and was on this earth way back when most people drove horse-drawn carriages. The railway then ran on steam and almost nobody had a telephone. "Such a nice, long life she had," people said.

However, Marie was very sad when she died. She was very, very fond of her great-grandmother.

Sometimes people pass away before they grow old, perhaps because they were ill or because they were in an accident. If you know the person and they have a place in your heart, the sadness is almost unbearable.

It hurts a lot, and it may feel as if this pain will never go away.

This is the case for everyone who experiences these things. In the moment, feels like we will never stop feeling such great sorrow. But that's the way it is

For some, it takes a while, and for others, it takes less time. As you know, everyone is different. And this is especially true when it comes to grief.

Some just sit there and don't want to eat, drink, or talk.

Others prefer to go for long walks.

Some busy themselves with work.

Just remember: there are many ways to be sad and each is fine!

At some point,
the terrible sorrow
lessens. Then you
begin to think more of
the nice things that you have
experienced with this person.

Marie remembers, for example, the way her
great-grandmother sang "Pop Goes the Weasel"
and how she sat on the bench and could say the
names of all the flowers and animals. And now Marie
knows that there is such a thing as a cuckoo flower and a
butterfly called a small tortoiseshell.

And when she sees all these things, then she is happy and feels as
though her great-grandmother is nearby. And her great-grandmother
would have been so happy to see her great-granddaughter so joyful.

No one who loves you would want you to be
sad forever.

When you're down, you could sing softly and
laugh and goof around. That's totally alright.

At first, when the pain is still so bad that you can hardly stand it, it's good to have a few things you can rely on. These recurring activities are called:

These also happen at some nice events: blowing out birthday cake candles, seeing fireworks on New Year's Eve, and throwing the bouquet at weddings are rituals. If you must see off a loved one, such rituals are particularly helpful.

People come together at funerals.

We lay flowers on graves.
There is coffee and cake.

Some people invent their
own rituals.

For you,
Grandpa!

Everyone is allowed
to mourn in their
own way, but it does
us good to have
something to which
we can hold tight.

I was at a funeral once. It was for a great-aunt I didn't know too well. Everyone was sad. But I didn't feel so sad. Is that bad?

No, not at all. A person can be sad, but nobody must be. Even if you had known your aunt better, it would be alright.

You can force yourself to be sad about as well as you can force yourself to have good luck. Perhaps the sad feelings did not come in time for the funeral.

It may be that these appear much later. Something may remind you of your loved one and then you may suddenly feel like crying.

Each person can mourn in their own way. There is no wrong way. And there is no right or wrong time to do it. So whatever you feel, and whenever you feel it, is fine.

The funeral for Marie's great-grandmother was a while ago.
Now Marie only sometimes has to cry a little, but even that is rare.
And she has begun to put together a book of all the flowers and
animals that she discovered with her great-grandmother. Sometimes
she even finds new ones that her great-grandmother might not
have known about. When Marie draws, she feels that her great-
grandmother is close to her and delights in her pretty pictures.

What Marie is doing is a ritual of remembrance. Everyone can come
up with different ways to think of a loved one.

It helps to remember them, and it's important to take time to do so.
But a person that means a lot is always with you, no matter where
they are now.